Instant Pot Recipe Collection

Flo Lum

PHOTOGRAPHS BY DUDE

For my YouTube Subscribers

Contents

Introduction

Pressure cooking has changed the way I prepare meals. I used to spend hours cooking meals on the stove, in the oven or in a slow cooker. Pressure cookers are time-savers for making recipes that would generally take a long and slow-cook process for tenderness and they are great at infusing flavours in a shorter time. I first learned how to use a pressure cooker in high school -- on one of those old school, stove top pots that whistled and jiggled. They were scary! I swore never to use one... ever!

Then, several years ago, I was looking for a new rice cooker with a stainless steel inner cooking pot. I was introduced to the Instant Pot, a multi-cooker, unlike the pressure cookers of the past. Convinced that it was safe, I decided to give it a try. After using it for a few weeks, I got rid of our rice cooker and our slow cooker, freeing up valuable counter space. That was short lived, however, as I ended up getting another Instant Pot! Now I have one Smart model and one DUO; both 6 quart size. So really, I didn't gain any space at all.

The recipes in this cookbook should work with other electric pressure cookers with similar features. If your electric pressure cooker does not have a sauté/browning function, you can sauté on the stovetop and transfer the ingredients to your pressure cooker.

Friends were often asking me for cooking tips and recipes. My husband thought it would be fun to share my tips and recipes online. Through his constant encouragement and support, I reluctantly allowed him to film and upload these videos to YouTube.

Now over 50,000 subscribers on my YouTube channel and with frequent nudging from my audience, I have compiled some of my favourite Instant Pot recipes into this book. These are tried and true recipes that I've tweaked along the way. My family loves them and I hope you and yours will love them too.

Thank you for letting me share a little bit of my simple, ordinary and joyful life and for welcoming me, through my recipes, into your home.

Acknowledgements

There are a few people I would like to acknowledge as I could not have done this on my own.

To my good friends, Allison Lau and Libby Yu, for taking time to help me edit this cookbook. Thank you!

To my husband, who always encourages and supports me, I thank you for believing in me and spurring me on to follow my passions.

To Ella and Noah, my beloved kidlets, who are the reason I do what I love and love what I do.

Sides

Mashed Potatoes

When I was in high school, one of my favourite menu items from the school cafeteria was mashed potatoes with gravy that only cost me $1. Thinking back, it was probably the most tasteless thing I could order. The mashed potatoes were made from the powdered stuff that came in a box and the gravy was incredibly bland, no doubt also made from some package.

I can assure you that this recipe is not that high school tragedy. Mashed potatoes are still one of my favourite sides but made with real potatoes, butter and cream. There is no comparison. I don't know what I was thinking.

Makes 4-6 servings

5-6 large whole russet potatoes
1 cup water
kosher salt
¼ cup butter
¼ cup half and half
1 tablespoon sour cream
salt and pepper

SIMPLE GRAVY (OPTIONAL)
¼ cup butter
¼ cup flour
1 cup beef broth
salt and pepper

---

1. Scrub potatoes well and place whole potatoes on a trivet in the inner cooking pot. Add 1 cup water and season with salt.

2. Close and lock the lid, making sure the steam knob is on Sealing/Locked. Pressure cook on high for 18 minutes.

3. Meanwhile, prepare the gravy. In a small pot, melt butter and stir in flour to make a roux. Cook for 1-2 minutes. Slowly add the broth and stir constantly until thickened. If it's too thick, add more broth. Season with salt and pepper if desired. Set aside until ready to serve.

4. Once the cooking is done, release the pressure by quick or natural pressure release.

5. Heat up the butter with the half and half in the microwave or on the stove.

6. Put the cooked potatoes in a medium mixing bowl and mash with a potato masher.

7. Add the melted butter and half and half to the potatoes and stir with a wooden spoon until the liquid has been absorbed. Add the sour cream and stir until incorporated.

8. Season with salt and pepper. Serve with gravy. It will also taste great without the gravy.

Killer Potato Salad

I have been making this potato salad since I was a teenager but it was my aunt who made it popular with our family; however, I don't remember if it was her recipe or mine? It's a side we delight in at our annual family Christmas potluck. But we also enjoy it in the summer at barbecues. In fact, it's great all year long!

Makes 6-8 servings

6 waxy potatoes (white, red or yukon), cut
    into 1 inch cubes
6 eggs
3 slices bacon, cooked and crumbled
1 celery stick, diced
½ carrot, slivered
2 green onions, chopped
1 cup mayonnaise
½ pound fresh cooked baby shrimp
salt and pepper

1. Pour 1 cup of water into the inner cooking pot. Put in a steamer basket and add the potatoes. Season with salt. Place the eggs on top.

2. Close and lock the lid, making sure the steam knob is on Sealing/Locked. Pressure cook on high for 6 minutes.

3. Once the cooking is done, quick release the pressure. Remove the eggs and place in an ice bath. Put the potatoes in a large mixing bowl. Cool potatoes for 20 - 30 minutes. Meanwhile, peel and chop the eggs then add to the potatoes.

4. Add bacon, celery, carrot, green onion, and mayonnaise and stir to combine. Fold in the shrimp. Salt and pepper to taste. Serve immediately while still warm or refrigerate until cold.

Smashed Potatoes

This is one of my kids' favourite sides. The boy, who dislikes potatoes in any form, will gobble these up. Perhaps it's the crispy texture on the outside that gives way to a creamy, buttery texture on the inside. When smashed potatoes joined the family menu rotation, I've noticed that we rarely have smashed potato leftovers.

Makes 2 servings

1 pound baby potatoes
½ cup water
3 tablespoons butter
salt and pepper

1. Place potatoes in a steamer basket in the inner cooking pot. Add water.

2. Close and lock the lid, making sure the steam knob is on Sealing/Locked. Pressure cook on high for 5 minutes.

3. Once the cooking is done, quick release the pressure.

4. Place the potatoes on a sheet pan. Flatten each potato with the back of a flat metal spatula. Spoon ½ teaspoon of butter onto each one and season with salt and pepper to taste.

5. Brown under the broiler for about 5-6 minutes.

6. Serve immediately.

Smashed Cheesy Potato Bites

These are smashed potatoes bumped up a couple of notches. They're a great party snack… bite-sized and topped with deliciousness. Growing up, one of my go-to appetizers to order was potato skins, made with unpeeled potato halves, hollowed and dressed with toppings like cheese, bacon and green onions. Smashed potatoes are my modern take on potato skins, made with less effort. Make them your own and experiment with your favourite toppings!

Makes 2 servings

1 pound baby potatoes
½ cup water
3 tablespoons butter
salt and pepper to taste
5 ounces marble cheddar cheese, grated
4-6 slices cooked bacon, crumbled
1 green onion, dark green parts only, chopped
sour cream (optional)

---

1. Place potatoes in a steamer basket in the inner cooking pot. Add water.

2. Close and lock the lid, making sure the steam knob is on Sealing/Locked. Pressure cook on high for 5 minutes.

3. Once the cooking is done, quick release the pressure.

4. Place the potatoes on a sheet pan. Flatten each potato with the back of a flat metal spatula. Spoon ½ teaspoon of butter onto each one and season with salt and pepper.

5. Brown under the broiler for about 5-6 minutes.

6. Top with cheese. Place under broiler for another minute or two until the cheese melts.

7. Finish them off by topping with bacon and green onion.

8. Enjoy with a dollop of sour cream.

Soups & Stews

Chicken Broth
Turkey Broth
Beef Bourguignon
Italian Bread Soup
Chili
Korean Beef Short Rib Soup (Galbi Tang)
Korean Braised Beef Short Ribs (Galbi Jjim)
Chicken Stew
Vietnamese Chicken Noodle Soup (Pho Ga)
Creamy Chicken and Gnocchi Soup
Pork Posole
Pork Stew
Salted Pork Congee
Zuppa Toscana
Bouillabaisse

Chicken Broth

This is a basic chicken broth that I make from all the roast chicken carcasses I save up in the freezer. It can be used right away in recipes or stored in smaller portions in the freezer.

Makes 8-10 cups

3 cooked chicken carcasses
1 tablespoon olive oil
2 tablespoons butter
1 medium onion, cut in half
1 carrot, cut in large pieces
1 celery stalk, cut in large pieces
2 sprigs fresh sage
4 sprigs fresh thyme
6 sprigs fresh Italian parsley
8 cups water
salt to taste

1. Tie the herbs together with kitchen string or twine to create an herb bouquet for easy removal.

2. Put all the ingredients into the inner cooking pot and cover with water filled to the 10 cup mark.

3. Close and lock the lid, making sure the steam knob is on Sealing/Locked. Pressure cook on high for 45 minutes.

4. Once the cooking is done, let it natural pressure release for about 15 minutes and then release the rest of the pressure by quick release.

5. Strain the broth through a sieve into a large bowl and skim the fat from the top. Use the stock in a soup recipe or freeze in small batches for future use.

Turkey Broth

Makes 8-10 cups

1 cooked turkey carcass
1 tablespoon olive oil
2 tablespoons butter
1 medium onion, cut in half
1 carrot, cut in large pieces
1 celery stalk, cut in large pieces
2 sprigs fresh sage
4 sprigs fresh thyme
6 sprigs fresh Italian parsley
8 cups water
salt to taste

1. Tie the herbs together with kitchen string or twine to create an herb bouquet for easy removal.

2. Put all the ingredients into the inner cooking pot and cover with water filled to the 10 cup mark.

3. Close and lock the lid, making sure the steam knob is on Sealing/Locked. Pressure cook on high for 45 minutes.

4. Once the cooking is done, let it natural pressure release for about 15 minutes and then release the rest of the pressure by quick release.

5. Strain the broth through a sieve into a large bowl and skim the fat from the top. Use the stock in a soup recipe or freeze in small batches for future use.

Beef Bourguignon

When I think of French cooking, the first thing that comes to mind is Julia Child and Boeuf Bourguignon. Using a pressure cooker makes this meal quicker to prepare.

While travelling in the South of France countryside, we stayed in a beautiful house in Bigorre, a tiny hamlet with a population of 13. There are only 7 houses there and the closest town is a 25-30 minute drive away.

Our hosts in the hamlet have an amazing vegetable garden where we harvested some carrots and herbs for our beef bourguignon. In my broken French, I gathered the courage to invite them to dinner. Seeing as they were French and well… I am not… why I chose to serve a French dish is beyond me. Thankfully, they enjoyed it!

Makes 6 servings

½ pound bacon, cut up into ½ inch pieces
olive oil
3 pounds boneless beef, cut into 2 inch cubes
1 cup flour
5 small shallots, sliced
5 medium carrots, cut into 1½-2 inch pieces
2-3 cloves garlic, minced
2 small onions, cut into quarters
6 sprigs fresh Italian parsley
4 sprigs fresh thyme
1 cup burgundy wine
1½ cup water
2 tablespoons tomato paste
salt and pepper
1 tablespoon butter
½ pound button or cremini, quartered
1 tablespoon chopped Italian parsley for garnish

1. Press Sauté, and adjust it to high heat. Once the pot is hot, add the bacon and render until brown.

2. Meanwhile, lightly coat the pieces of beef in the flour. Remove the bacon and drain on a paper towel.

3. Add some olive oil to the inner cooking pot if needed. In small batches, brown the

meat on each side. Be careful not to overcrowd the meat so that they brown properly. Remove the meat into a bowl.

4. Add more olive oil to the inner cooking pot if needed. Then add the shallots, carrots and onion and sauté them for a few minutes. Add the garlic and stir for another 30 seconds.

5. Pour in the wine to deglaze, scraping up the brown bits from the bottom of the pot as you go. Let the wine cook for few minutes to burn off the alcohol.

6. Cancel Sauté mode. Return the meat and any drippings to the pot. Add the tomato paste, parsley, thyme, water, salt and pepper.

7. Close and lock the lid, making sure the steam knob is on Sealing/Locked. Pressure cook on high for 45 minutes.

8. Meanwhile, heat up a frying pan on medium heat. Melt the butter and add the mushrooms, toss lightly. Let the mushroom brown without stirring by allowing the liquid to burn off. Once all the liquid is gone and the mushrooms start to turn golden brown, add salt and then give it a stir. Remove from heat until needed.

9. Once the cooking is done, release the pressure by quick or natural pressure release.

10. Stir in the mushrooms. Garnish with chopped parsley. Serve with fresh bread.

Italian Bread Soup

It is interesting to me to see the variety of soups from different cultures. This Italian soup uses stale bread as a thickener. The texture reminds me of congee, Asian rice porridge. This is definitely a filling one-pot meal.

Makes 6-8 servings

½ pound pancetta or thick bacon,
    cut into small pieces
3 large carrots, diced
1 medium onion, diced
2 celery stalks, diced
3 cloves garlic, minced
salt and pepper
2 bay leaves
4 fresh basil leaves, chopped
28 ounce can diced tomatoes
2 15 ounce cans cannellini beans, rinsed
    and drained
5-6 cups chicken broth

small bunch kale, leaves removed from
    the stem and chopped
½ loaf of stale white country bread or
    French bread
½ cup freshly grated Parmesan cheese

1. Press Sauté, and adjust it to high heat. Once the pot is hot, add the bacon and render until brown. Remove the bacon and drain on a paper towel.

2. Leave 2 tablespoons of bacon fat in the pot and add the carrots, onion, and celery to pot to cook until soft, about 5 minutes. Add garlic and cook 30 seconds to 1 min. Season with salt and pepper.

3. Cancel Sauté mode. Add bay leaves, basil, tomatoes, beans and 5 cups chicken broth.

4. Close and lock the lid, making sure the steam knob is on Sealing/Locked. Pressure cook on high for 10 minutes.

5. Meanwhile, cut up the bread into 1 inch cubes.

6. Once the cooking is done, release the pressure by quick or natural pressure release.

7. Turn on Sauté. When the soup begins to simmer, add the kale, bread and cheese. If there isn't enough liquid, add more chicken broth until desired consistency. Season with salt and pepper as needed.

8. Serve soup garnished with bacon bits.

Chili

There are so many different ways to make chili. Every family probably has their own version to suit their tastes. This is my version which has become a family favourite. It's easy and we enjoy it especially on cold, wet days -- we get a lot of those here in Vancouver.

Makes 6 servings

2 tablespoons vegetable or canola oil
1 medium onion, chopped
2 cloves garlic, minced
1½ pound lean ground beef
1 teaspoon kosher salt
1 teaspoon dried oregano
1 teaspoon ground cumin
2 tablespoons chili powder
1 tablespoon dried parsley
1 teaspoon ground black pepper
1 teaspoon cayenne pepper (optional)
1 cup water
1 pound cooked sausage, diced
  (e.g. garlic or Ukrainian or chorizo)

15 ounce can red kidney beans, rinsed
  and drained
15 ounce can pinto beans, rinsed and
  drained
4 ounce can mild diced green chilies
2 tablespoons tomato paste
28 ounce can diced tomatoes
6 ounces grated Monterey Jack cheese
  (for garnish)
1 tablespoon chopped cilantro (for
  garnish)

1. Press Sauté. Once the pot is hot, heat oil and add the onions. Sauté the onions for 3-5 minutes until softened. Add garlic, cook for 30 seconds or until fragrant.

2. Cancel Sauté mode and press Sauté again, adjust it to high heat. Add ground beef and cook until brown. Stir in the spices.

3. Cancel Sauté mode. Add the following ingredients in order: water, sausage, beans, green chilies, tomato paste, and tomatoes. Do not stir.

4. Close and lock the lid, making sure the steam knob is on Sealing/Locked. Pressure cook on manual high pressure for 10 minutes.

5. Once the cooking is done, release the pressure by quick or natural pressure release.

6. Garnish with grated Monterey Jack cheese and chopped cilantro.

Korean Beef Short Rib Soup (Galbi Tang)

Korean soup is super comforting to me. It's both hearty and delicate in flavour. This soup is made with simple ingredients that come together in a delicious and flavourful meal.

Makes 6-8 servings

2 pounds bone-in beef short ribs
1 medium onion, sliced
1 small daikon, sliced into ¼ inch semi-circles
8 cups water
3 cloves garlic, minced
7 ounces potato starch noodles
salt to taste
2 eggs, lightly beaten
2 green onions chopped

———

1. Rinse the short ribs and soak them in cold water for about an hour to remove excess blood and impurities. Bring a large pot of water to boil. Give the ribs another rinse then add them to the boiling water and boil them for 10 minutes. This method is called parboiling which will release more impurities from the bones, giving you a clearer broth. Drain and rinse the ribs under cold water.

2. Add the ribs, onion, daikon and water to the inner cooking pot.

3. Close and lock the lid, making sure the steam knob is on Sealing/Locked. Pressure cook on high for 30 minutes.

4. Once the cooking is done, release the pressure by quick or natural pressure release.

5. Skim the fat from the top. Press Sauté and add garlic and noodles. Cook for 8 minutes. Season with salt.

6. Cancel Sauté mode. Slowly stream the egg into the soup while stirring to create egg ribbons.

7. Garnish with green onions and serve with Japanese rice.

Korean Braised Beef Short Ribs (Galbi Jjim)

The first time I tried Galbi Jjim, it was served in a huge pot, family style. It also came with several little Korean sides (Banchan) that is included with your meal, adding a variety of flavours and textures. It was so incredibly delicious, I had to replicate it at home!

Makes 6 servings

3 pounds bone-in beef short ribs
1 cup beef broth
3 tablespoons soy sauce
1 tablespoon brown sugar
1 tablespoon rice wine
1 tablespoon sesame oil
2 tablespoon light corn syrup
6 cloves garlic, minced
1 small onion, thinly sliced
3 carrots, cut into 1½-2 inch pieces

3 white potatoes, peeled and cut into
   1½-2 inch pieces
2 green onions, chopped

We often have prime rib for large family gatherings and I will save the cooked bones for making Galbi Jjim. I love the added flavour from the roast.

1. Rinse the short ribs and soak them in cold water for about an hour to remove excess blood and impurities. Bring a large pot of water to boil. Give the ribs another rinse then add them to the boiling water and boil them for 10 minutes. This method is called parboiling which will release more impurities from the bones giving you a clearer broth. Drain and rinse the ribs under cold water.

2. Combine beef broth, soy sauce, brown sugar, rice wine, sesame oil, corn syrup and garlic in a large measuring cup. Stir until brown sugar is dissolved.

3. In the inner cooking pot, add rib bones, onion, carrots, and potatoes. Pour the sauce over the top.

4. Close and lock the lid, making sure the steam knob is on Sealing/Locked. Pressure cook on high for 45 minutes.

5. Once the cooking is done, release the pressure by quick or natural pressure release.

6. Remove the short ribs and vegetables to a plate. Press Sauté, and adjust it to high heat to reduce sauce until thickened, about 8 minutes.

7. Pour the sauce over the beef and vegetables, sprinkle green onion on top. Serve with rice and kimchi.

Chicken Stew

I remember when microwaves first came out. My family owned a grocery store and we had a microwave available for customers' use. One of the first things I 'nuked' was a frozen pot pie. That's what chicken stew reminded me of: The inside of a chicken pot pie.

But this is so much better! This is one of those comfort foods that makes me feel warm and cozy, especially on cold, rainy days. I love the richness of the gravy and homey flavours. No more nuking pot pies in the microwave.

Makes 4-6 servings

1 tablespoon vegetable or canola oil
8 skin-on, bone-in chicken thighs
salt and pepper
2 tablespoons butter
4 small carrots, diced
2 medium onion, diced
2 celery stalks, diced
¼ cup flour
2 cups chicken broth
2 sprigs of fresh thyme or ½ teaspoon dried thyme
1 cup whipping cream
1 cup frozen peas
1 tablespoon fresh chopped Italian parsley, extra for garnish

———

1. Press Sauté, and adjust it to high heat. Season the skin of the chicken thighs with salt and pepper. Once the pot is hot, heat oil and add the chicken skin side down. Season the side facing up with salt and pepper. To avoid overcrowding the chicken, cook the chicken in two batches. Brown for 2-3 minutes on each side and remove to a plate. Repeat with the second batch.

2. Cancel Sauté mode. Leave 2 tablespoons of chicken fat in the pot. Turn on Sauté mode. Add butter.

3. Add the carrots, onion, and celery and sauté until soft, about 5 minutes. Season with salt and pepper.

4. Add flour and sauté for another minute. Add 1 cup chicken broth and scrape the bottom of the pot to deglaze, scraping up the brown bits from the bottom of the pot as you go.

5. Cancel Sauté mode. Add the chicken, drippings and remaining chicken broth. Close and lock the lid, making sure the steam knob is on Sealing/Locked. Pressure cook on high for 8 minutes.

6. Once the cooking is done, release the pressure by quick or natural pressure release.

7. Turn on Sauté. When the soup begins to simmer, add whipping cream. Stir and bring to simmer. Season with more salt and pepper if needed. Stir in peas and simmer until heated through.

8. Serve stew in a bowl with a side of mashed potatoes or with biscuits and garnish with parsley.

Vietnamese Chicken Noodle Soup (Pho Ga)

When we lived in San Francisco, there was a Vietnamese restaurant we used to frequent. Even now, whenever we visit, we have to eat there at least once.

At the time, we were most familiar with ordering beef noodle soup (Pho Bo). But this particular restaurant served a large variety of dishes and soups we had never had before. This is where we were introduced to Pho Ga. While we love a good bowl of pho bo, the lighter flavour of the pho ga was a refreshing change.

Makes 4 servings

2 tablespoons vegetable or canola oil
2 medium onions, halved
3 ounce piece of ginger, sliced
3-4 pound whole chicken
1 bunch cilantro
2 star anise
1 tablespoon rock sugar
4 whole cloves
½ teaspoon ground coriander (or 1 teaspoon whole coriander)
1 cinnamon stick
1 teaspoon kosher salt
8 cups water

TO SERVE
1 pound rice stick noodles, cooked following package instructions
4 green onion, chopped
½ bunch cilantro, chopped
½ pound bean sprouts
4 stems Thai basil
4 Thai chili peppers
½ lime cut into 4 wedges
Hoisin sauce
Sriracha sauce

1. Press Sauté and adjust it to high heat. Once the pot is hot, heat the oil, add the onion and ginger, and char both sides until blackened. This will take about 5-10 minutes. Cancel Sauté mode.

2. Add the chicken, cilantro, star anise, rock sugar, cloves, coriander, cinnamon and

salt. Cover all the ingredients with water making sure the water level does not go over the 10 cup mark on the inner pot.

3. Close and lock the lid, making sure the steam knob is on Sealing/Locked. Pressure cook on high pressure for 25 minutes.

4. In the meantime, prepare the remaining ingredients.

5. Once the cooking is done, let the pressure naturally release for at least 15 minutes before quick releasing the rest of the pressure.

6. Skim the fat from the top. Take the chicken out, remove the skin and bones, shred the meat.

7. Divide the noodles equally in four individual serving bowls, and top with some of the chicken, green onion, cilantro, and bean sprouts. Pour in hot soup and serve with the remaining ingredients.

Creamy Chicken & Gnocchi Soup

Makes 6-8 servings

8 slices bacon, cut into ½ inch pieces
3 small carrots, diced
1 medium onion, diced
2 celery stalks, diced
2 cloves garlic, minced
salt and pepper
6 skin-on, bone-in chicken thighs
6 cups water
1½ pound gnocchi
1 cup whipping cream
1 tablespoon fresh chopped Italian
    parsley, extra for garnish
2 cups fresh spinach

Instead of chicken thighs and water, you can substitute chicken broth and once the soup is done cooking, add shredded pre-cooked chicken.

1.   Press Sauté, and adjust it to high heat. Once the pot is hot, add the bacon and render until brown. Remove the bacon and drain on a paper towel.

2.   Leave 2 tablespoons of bacon fat in the pot and add the carrots, onion, and celery to pot to cook until soft, about 5 minutes. Add garlic and cook 30 seconds to 1 min. Season with salt and pepper.

3.   Cancel Sauté mode. Add chicken thighs. Add enough water to just cover the ingredients. Close and lock the lid, making sure the steam knob is on Sealing/Locked. Pressure cook on high for 10 minutes.

4.   Meanwhile, on the stove, bring a large pot of water to boil. Cook gnocchi according to directions on the package. Set aside until ready to use.

5.   Once the soup is done cooking, release the pressure by quick or natural pressure release. Take the chicken out, remove the skin and bones, shred the meat and add the meat back to the pot.

6.   Skim the fat from the top. Turn on Sauté. When the soup begins to simmer, add whipping cream to the pot. Stir and bring to a simmer. Season with more salt and pepper as needed. Stir in chopped Italian parsley, fresh spinach, and gnocchi. Stir and simmer until heated through.

7.   Serve soup in bowl and garnish with extra parsley and bacon bits.

Pork Posole

Having lived in California, there was a large selection of authentic Mexican restaurants to choose from. In Canada, we don't have as much variety but it is getting better. There are more authentic Mexican restaurants popping up.

This is not authentic pork posole but I think it comes close to the flavours I remember. At the very least, it's a pork soup that has Mexican elements.

Makes 6-8 servings

3 pounds pork shoulder, cut into 2 inch pieces
1 medium onion, cut into quarters
6 cloves garlic, smashed
1 bay leaf
5 teaspoons dried oregano
2 teaspoons ground cumin
2 teaspoons kosher salt
8 cups water
4 ounce can diced green chilies
1 cup frozen corn
15 ounce can black beans, rinsed
    and drained
¼ cup sour cream
1 tablespoon cilantro
1 avocado, sliced
tortilla chips for garnish

---

1. In the inner cooking pot, add pork, onion, garlic, bay leaf, oregano, cumin, salt and cover with water.

2. Close and lock the lid, making sure the steam knob is on Sealing/Locked. Pressure cook on high for 45 minutes.

3. Once the cooking is done, release the pressure by quick or natural pressure release.

4. Skim the fat from the top.

5. Press Sauté, add the chilies, corn and black beans. Heat through.

6. Garnish with a spoonful of sour cream, cilantro, avocado and tortilla chips.

Pork Stew

I'm a big believer in using what I have at home. I don't always have the option of going to the market at the last minute to get groceries for dinner. Keeping my pantry stocked with the basics and having some meat in the freezer comes in very handy.

One day, I had absolutely no idea what we were going to have for dinner. I found a pork shoulder in the freezer and grabbed whatever I could find in my fridge and pantry. This was the result and it turned out so well that it has become a regular dish on our family menu.

Makes 6-8 servings

3 pounds pork shoulder, cut into 2 inch
    cubes (fresh or frozen)
2 medium onions, quartered
4 carrots, cut into large pieces
2 cloves garlic, minced
½ cup chicken broth
1 28 ounce can diced tomatoes
1 tablespoon tomato paste
1 teaspoon dried oregano
salt and pepper
1 tablespoon chopped Italian parsley

1. In the inner cooking pot, add all the ingredients.

2. Close and lock the lid, making sure the steam knob is on Sealing/Locked. Pressure cook on high for 45 minutes.

3. Once the cooking is done, release the pressure by quick or natural pressure release.

4. Skim the fat from the top.

5. Garnish with parsley. Serve with rice or a fresh loaf of bread.

By freezing pork shoulder already cut up into 2 inch cubes, will save you time, as they will be ready to use. A whole frozen roast will take much longer to defrost, in order to cut up into cubes.

Salted Pork Congee

Congee is an Asian comfort food. Generally, people have it for breakfast or brunch. It is also popular as a part of a late night meal when served with tasty side dishes like deep-fried salt and pepper fishies, squid or tofu.

It is also often made when someone is sick. So for me, it's comfort food. My kids associate it with "sick" food, not comforting at all. They will enjoy it with all the deep fried sides mentioned above though.

Makes 6-8 servings

2 pounds pork neck bones
2 tablespoons kosher salt
water
1¾ cup rice
½ teaspoon kosher salt
½ teaspoon vegetable or canola oil
1 tablespoon chopped green onions for garnish
½ teaspoon sesame oil
pinch of ground white pepper

———

1. Place the bones in a medium bowl and sprinkle liberally with salt. Marinate 24-48 hours, covered in the refrigerator.

2. Bring a large pot of water to boil. Give the ribs a rinse then add them to the boiling water and boil them for 10 minutes. This method is called parboiling which will release more impurities from the bones giving you a clearer broth. Drain and rinse the ribs under cold water.

3. Place the bones in the inner cooking pot and add enough water to cover but do not fill above the 10 cup mark.

4. Close and lock the lid, making sure the steam knob is on Sealing/Locked. Pressure cook on high for 45 minutes.

5. Meanwhile, rinse the rice in a sieve and then put it in a small mixing bowl. Add the salt and oil and marinate for at least 30 minutes.

6. Once the cooking is done, release the pressure by quick or natural pressure release.

7. Remove the bones and set aside. Add the rice to the pork broth. Add more water if

necessary to reach the 10 cup mark.

8. Close and lock the lid, making sure the steam knob is on Sealing/Locked. Pressure cook on low for 20 minutes.

9. Meanwhile remove the pork from the bones and shred the meat.

10. Once the cooking is done, let it natural pressure release for about 15 minutes and then release the rest of the pressure by quick release.

11. Give the congee a good stir and add the shredded pork.

12. Serve in a bowl and garnish with green onions, sesame oil and white pepper.

Zuppa Toscana

This is a super easy and delicious soup recipe that our family loves. It's a replica of the one you can get at that well-known Italian restaurant chain and it's so easy to make, you can have it anytime!

Makes 6-8 servings

4 slices of bacon, cut into small pieces
1 pound mild Italian sausage meat
1 medium onion, chopped
2 cloves garlic, minced
4 medium red potatoes, sliced into ¼ inch semi-circles
pinch crushed red pepper flakes
6 cups chicken broth
3 cups chopped kale
1 cup whipping cream
salt and pepper to taste

———

1. Press Sauté, and adjust it to high heat. Once the pot is hot, add the bacon and render until brown. Remove the bacon and drain on a paper towel.

2. Add chopped onion to the pot and sauté them for a few minutes. Add the garlic and stir for another 30 seconds. Add the sausage meat and brown until cooked.

3. Add the sliced potatoes. Cover with the chicken broth. Close and lock the lid, making sure the steam knob is on Sealing/Locked. Pressure cook on high for 8 minutes.

4. Once the cooking is done, release the pressure by quick or natural pressure release.

5. Press Sauté and add the kale and whipping cream. Heat through. Salt and pepper to taste.

6. Serve with fresh crusty bread.

Bouillabaisse

The first time I had bouillabaisse, the description from the menu looked delicious. When the dish was set down before me, I was shocked to see there were only five tiny pieces of seafood sitting in a thin layer of broth. Suffice it to say, it was not a satisfying meal and it was expensive.

Having lived on the west coast most of my life, seafood is always fresh and readily available. You too, can make this French seafood stew at home at a much lower cost than ordering it at a fancy restaurant. It is definitely a wonderful meal to share with great company. Pair the stew with a quality baguette and your guests won't go home hungry.

Makes 6-8 servings

2 tablespoons olive oil
1 medium onion, sliced
½ fennel, sliced
1 leek, sliced
2 cloves garlic, minced
½ teaspoon saffron threads
3 pieces of orange zest, 2 inch strips
14 ounce can whole tomatoes

4 cups fish or vegetable stock
salt and pepper
3 pounds wild cod or any fish cut into 2
    inch pieces
12 large scallops (defrosted if frozen)
12 large prawns (defrosted if frozen)
1 pound fresh cooked crab meat
1 tablespoon Italian parsley

---

1. Press Sauté. Once the pot is hot, heat oil and add onion, fennel, leek and garlic. Sauté for 10 minutes or until they start to brown.

2. Cancel Sauté mode. Use a vegetable peeler to create orange zest strips. Add saffron, orange zest, tomatoes, stock, salt and pepper.

3. Close and lock the lid, making sure the steam knob is on Sealing/Locked. Pressure cook on high for 10 minutes.

4. Once the cooking is done, release the pressure by quick or natural pressure release.

5. Press Sauté, remove the orange strips, break up tomatoes if necessary and add seafood except crabmeat and cook for 4 minutes. Add crabmeat and heat through.

6. Garnish with Italian parsley. Serve in a large bowl with fresh bread.

Mains

Easy Pot Roast

I used to use the slow cooker out of convenience, but I often found meat was dry or over-cooked. After I discovered pressure cooking, I adapted my slow cooker recipes for the electric pressure cooker. When you're strapped for time, the Instant Pot is easy and faster than slow cooking, with consistent results. This pot roast is simple and delicious and the meat is tender and moist. Hope you find it to be as well.

Makes 4-6 servings

1 tablespoon vegetable or canola oil
2 pounds bottom round or chuck roast
1 large onion, halved
6 carrots, cut into 2 inch pieces
½ cup beef broth
1 teaspoon dried thyme
salt to taste

---

1. Press Sauté and adjust to high heat. Once the pot is hot, add the oil. Liberally salt all sides of your pot roast. Brown the roast about 2-3 minutes per side. Remove the roast onto a plate and set aside.

2. Add onion and carrots and sauté for a few minutes. Add the beef broth to deglaze, scraping up the brown bits from the bottom of the pot as you go.

3. Cancel Sauté mode. Remove some of the vegetables to make room to add the roast to the bottom of the pot. Put the vegetables back in.

4. Sprinkle with thyme and salt to taste.

5. Close and lock the lid, making sure the steam knob is on Sealing/Locked. Pressure cook on high for 45 minutes.

6. Once the cooking is done, release the pressure by quick or natural pressure release.

7. Serve with rice or mashed potatoes.

Beef & Broccoli

This is a one-pot meal using the pot-in-pot method. Perfect for getting dinner ready quickly with less to clean up.

Makes 4 servings

1 tablespoon fresh ginger, grated
1 clove garlic, minced
1 shallot, sliced
1 pound top sirloin or flank steak, cut into thin strips
2 tablespoons soy sauce
¼ cup water
1 teaspoon sugar

1 pinch kosher salt
1 cup rice, rinsed
1 cup water
1 pound broccoli, cut into sections
1 teaspoon cornstarch
1 teaspoon cool water

1. Press Sauté, and adjust it to high heat. Once the pot is hot, add oil, ginger, garlic, and shallots. Cook for about 1 minute until fragrant. Add the beef and cook for 1-2 minutes.

2. Cancel Sauté mode. Add soy sauce, ¼ cup water, sugar and salt to the beef.

3. Place trivet over meat. Put the rice and water into a 3 cup, oven safe bowl that will fit into the inner cooking pot and place onto the trivet.

4. Close and lock the lid, making sure the steam knob is on Sealing/Locked. Pressure cook on high for 4 minutes.

5. Once the cooking is done, quick release the pressure.

6. Remove bowl of rice and cover with a lid or clean towel to steam for 10 minutes. Remove trivet and add broccoli.

7. Close and lock the lid, making sure the steam knob is on Sealing/Locked. Pressure cook on high for 0 (zero) minutes.

8. Once the cooking is done, quick release the pressure.

9. Press Sauté to simmer the sauce. In a small bowl, dissolve the cornstarch in the water and stir the slurry into the sauce. Heat through until sauce thickens. If it's not thick enough, add another mixture of slurry.

10. Serve over rice.

Tomato & Beef

I have fond memories of weekly visits to my grandparents' house. Every week for dinner, grandma would make tomato and beef on rice. You'd think I would have grown tired of this dish but it's actually one of my all time favourites! I can still hear my grandma's voice telling me how to make it with "just a bit of this and bit of that." It makes me happy that tomato and beef has also become a favourite for my own family.

Makes 4-6 servings

1 tablespoon vegetable or canola oil
2 medium onions, sliced
3 slices of ginger, approx 2 inches long
4 green onion, cut into 2 inch pieces, separating the white and green parts
2 pounds tomatoes, cut into pieces or 28 ounce can whole tomatoes
1 pound lean ground beef

1 teaspoon kosher salt
3 tablespoons soy sauce
1 tablespoon dark soy sauce
1 tablespoon oyster sauce
1 tablespoon sugar
3 tablespoons ketchup
1 tablespoon cornstarch
1 tablespoon cold water

1. Press Sauté. Once the pot is hot, add the oil. Sauté the onion, white parts of the green onion, and ginger for 2-3 minutes. Add the ground beef and brown until cooked through.

2. Cancel sauté mode. Add the tomatoes, salt, soy sauce, dark soy sauce, oyster sauce, sugar and ketchup.

3. Close and lock the lid, making sure the steam knob is on Sealing/Locked. Pressure cook on high for 5 minutes.

4. Once the cooking is done, release the pressure by quick or natural pressure release.

5. Press Sauté to simmer the sauce. In a small bowl, dissolve the cornstarch in the water and stir the slurry into the sauce. Heat through until sauce thickens.

6. Add the green parts of the green onion and heat through.

7. Serve with rice.

Braised Beef Short Ribs

I love the tenderness of beef short ribs and the sauce that comes with it and I often serve it with mashed potatoes. This recipe is another example of how an electric pressure cooker excels at infusing flavours into a dish in a shorter amount of time.

Makes 6 servings

1 cup flour
1 teaspoon kosher salt
½ teaspoon pepper
3 pounds boneless beef short ribs, cut into 3 inch pieces
8 slices bacon, cut into small pieces
1 medium onion
3 small carrots
3 celery stalks
1 tomato
4 cloves garlic
2 teaspoons dried thyme
¾ cup red wine
½ cup beef broth
1 tablespoon Italian parsley, chopped

---

1. In a medium shallow dish, combine flour, salt and pepper.

2. With a paper towel, pat dry the meat. Dredge the meat in the flour mixture and set aside.

3. Press Sauté and adjust it to high heat. Once the pot is hot, add the bacon and render until brown. Remove the bacon and drain on a paper towel.

4. Brown the short ribs for 2 minutes on each side in the bacon fat.

5. Meanwhile, in a food processor, add the onion, carrots, celery, tomato and garlic and purée.

6. Remove the meat from the pot and set aside on a clean plate. Add thyme, vegetable purée and cook for a couple of minutes.

7. Pour in the wine to deglaze, scraping up the brown bits from the bottom of the pot as you go. Let the wine cook for few minutes to burn off the alcohol. Cancel Sauté mode.

8. Return the short ribs with drippings to the pot and add the broth.

9. Close and lock the lid, making sure the steam knob is on Sealing/Locked. Pressure cook on high for 45 minutes.

10. Once the cooking is done, release the pressure by quick or natural pressure release.

11. Place the short ribs on a serving platter. Skim the fat from the top. Press Sauté and reduce the sauce to your desired consistency. Pour sauce over the short ribs. Garnish with Italian parsley and bacon bits.

Chicken Shawarma

Surprisingly, my favourite meal in Paris, France was chicken shawarma. We had arrived quite late in the evening and found a restaurant where we were able to get take out. I have had chicken shawarma before but this was truly the best I had ever tasted. All the flavours exploded in my mouth! When I'm reminiscent of our wonderful time in Paris, I enjoy making this dish.

Makes 6-8 servings

3 pounds boneless, skinless chicken thighs
1 medium onion, quartered
1 tablespoon Italian parsley, chopped (garnish)

MARINADE
¼ cup fresh lemon juice
4 cloves garlic, minced
2 teaspoon paprika
2 teaspoon ground cumin
½ teaspoon turmeric
pinch of ground cinnamon
pinch of crushed chili flakes
1 teaspoon kosher salt
ground pepper to taste
½ cup olive oil

WHITE SAUCE
¼ cup tahini
2 tablespoon water, more as needed
1 clove garlic, minced (add more if desired)
1½ tablespoon lemon juice
2 pinches kosher salt

---

1. Place all the marinade ingredients into a gallon sized resealable bag. Add the chicken thighs, making sure the marinade is coating each piece. Refrigerate for at least 30 minutes to 2 hours.

2. In the inner cooking pot, add onion and pour in the marinade and chicken.

3. Close and lock the lid, making sure the steam knob is on Sealing/Locked. Pressure cook on high for 8 minutes.

4. Meanwhile, make the white sauce. In a small bowl, combine white sauce ingredients and mix well. Start with 2 tablespoons of water and add more if needed. You should be able to drizzle the sauce.

5. Once the cooking is done, release the pressure by quick pressure release.

6. Preheat the broiler and transfer the chicken pieces onto a sheet pan. Broil until browned, about 3 minutes. Alternatively, pan fry in a hot frying pan or brown on the grill.

7. Place the chicken on a serving platter, drizzle with white sauce and garnish with chopped Italian parsley. Serve with rice and hummus.

Malaysian Curry Chicken

I love how there are so many different styles and flavours of curry. Dude's family is from Malaysia so it's been great learning about this style of cooking over the years. I especially like the flavours and fragrances of lemongrass and lime leaves. One of the ways I tried to win my husband's heart was by learning how to cook Malaysian food. What a fool I was, trying to impress him when really... he should have been impressing me.

My mother-in-law no longer makes her own curry pastes from scratch and has gone to packaged pastes. There are some really good ones on the market now. We like Tean's Gourmet brand.

Makes 6-8 servings

1 tablespoon vegetable or canola oil
12 skin-on, bone-in chicken thighs
1 medium onion, sliced
6 potatoes, chopped into 1½ - 2 inch pieces
½ to 1 package Tean's Gourmet Chicken Curry paste
½ cup water
13.5 ounce can coconut milk

———

1. Press Sauté and adjust it to high heat. Once the pot is hot, add the oil. Brown 4-5 chicken thighs, skin side down for about 3-4 minutes. Turn them over and brown the other side for 3-4 minutes. Remove them onto a plate and set aside. Repeat with remaining chicken. You will need to do this in a couple of batches.

2. Add the sliced onion and sauté them for a few minutes, scraping up the brown bits from the bottom of the pot as you go. You can add a couple of tablespoons of water to make deglazing easier.

3. Add the potatoes and place the chicken on top. Cancel Sauté mode.

4. Mix ½ to 1 whole package of paste in the water depending on how spicy you like it. Stir in the coconut milk. Pour this mixture over the chicken.

5. Close and lock the lid, making sure the steam knob is on Sealing/Locked. Pressure cook on high for 8 minutes.

6. Once the cooking is done, release the pressure by quick or natural pressure release.

7. Serve with jasmine rice.

Fast Roast Chicken

Roast chicken is a staple dish in our family, well suited to our meat-loving kids. When roasting a chicken in the oven, I turn the chicken to evenly roast on each side, which is why I have chosen to brown the chicken on all sides in this recipe. Roast chicken makes a great meal but the leftovers are also handy for sandwiches, soups or stews. One chicken can be stretched or transformed into multiple meals during the week, making menu planning a little simpler.

Makes 4-6 servings

1 tablespoon vegetable or canola oil
1 tablespoon butter
3 pound whole chicken
salt and pepper
4 sprigs fresh thyme or 1 teaspoon dried thyme
1 bulb garlic, cut in half
1 lemon, cut in half
¼ cup water

———————

1. Press Sauté and adjust it to high heat. Once the pot is hot, add the oil and butter.

2. Season the breast side of the chicken with salt and pepper. Brown the chicken breast side down. Salt and pepper the back side of the chicken. Brown on all 4 sides for about 2 minutes per side, browning the back side last.

3. Place the thyme and garlic inside the cavity of the chicken. Squeeze the lemon juice over the chicken and put the lemon halves into the cavity as well. Cancel Sauté mode.

4. Add water. Close and lock the lid, making sure the steam knob is on Sealing/Locked. Pressure cook on high for 17 minutes (or 5.5 minutes per pound of chicken).

5. Once the cooking is done, quick release the pressure

6. To crisp the skin, you can put the chicken under the broiler for a few minutes or put it in a preheated 425°F oven for 10 minutes.

Butter Chicken

Butter chicken was probably my very first taste of Indian cuisine. It is now one of the kids' favourite dishes to order at an Indian restaurant. For many years, I was intimidated by Indian cooking; maybe it was the unfamiliar spices. I eventually took a basic Indian cooking class and discovered it was \not as difficult as I thought. This recipe has been a wonderful introduction to cooking Indian cuisine at home and has become a family favourite.

Makes 4 servings

¼ cup vegetable or canola oil
6 cloves garlic, minced
1 tablespoon fresh ginger, grated
5.5 ounce can tomato paste
1 teaspoon kosher salt
1 tablespoon paprika
1 teaspoon ground cumin
1 teaspoon turmeric
1 teaspoon ground coriander
2 teaspoon garam masala
½ cup chicken broth
1 pound boneless, skinless chicken thighs or breasts, cut into bite size pieces
1½ cup whipping cream
1 tablespoon fresh cilantro, chopped for garnish

———

1. Press Sauté and adjust it to low heat. Once the pot is hot, add the oil and garlic. Stir until the garlic is a bit sticky and starting to brown. Add the ginger and cook for 30 seconds.

2. Add tomato paste and cook for 1 minute. Stir in all the spices and cook for about 4 minutes. Cancel Sauté mode.

3. Stir in chicken broth and chicken.

4. Close and lock the lid, making sure the steam knob is on Sealing/Locked. Pressure cook on high for 5 minutes.

5. Once the cooking is done, release the pressure by quick or natural pressure release.

6. Press Sauté and add whipping cream. Cook until heated through.

7. Garnish with cilantro. Serve with basmati rice.

Teriyaki Chicken

Yes, you can buy teriyaki sauce in a bottle but why when you can make your own. By having the basic sauces on hand you can create a lot of sauces from scratch and it only takes a few extra minutes.

Makes 6-8 servings

3 pounds skin-on, bone-in chicken thighs
½ cup soy sauce
¼ cup Mirin sauce
1 tablespoon rice vinegar
1 teaspoon sesame oil
2 tablespoons brown sugar
2 teaspoons grated fresh ginger
2 cloves garlic minced
3 pounds skin-on, bone-in chicken thighs
2 tablespoon cornstarch
1 tablespoon cold water

1. In the inner cooking pot, combine the chicken thighs, soy sauce, Mirin, vinegar, sesame oil, brown sugar, ginger, and garlic.

2. Close and lock the lid, making sure the steam knob is on Sealing/Locked. Pressure cook on high for 8 minutes.

3. Once the cooking is done, release the pressure by quick or natural pressure release.

4. Place chicken on a baking sheet. Baste chicken with the sauce from the pot and broil for 3-5 minutes until skin is crispy and starting to caramelize.

5. Press Sauté to simmer the sauce. In a small bowl, dissolve the cornstarch in the water and stir the slurry into the sauce. Heat through until sauce thickens. If it's not thick enough, add another mixture of slurry.

6. Spoon sauce over the chicken and serve with Japanese rice.

Chicken Adobo

One of our favourite dishes is Filipino chicken adobo. Dude especially likes the vinegar in it and if it was up to him, he'd want to double the amount I use. There are many versions of this recipe but the common ingredients in most recipes are soy sauce, vinegar, peppercorn and bay leaves. I've adapted my version for the Instant Pot. It's easy and delicious. I hope you'll enjoy it.

Makes 6-8 servings

3 pounds skin-on, bone-in chicken thighs
6 tablespoons soy sauce
5 cloves garlic, smashed
¼ cup vegetable or canola oil
1 tablespoons sugar
¼ cup vinegar
2 bay leaves
1 teaspoon whole peppercorn
¼ cup water

---

1. Place the chicken, soy sauce, and garlic in a large resealable bag. Marinate in the fridge for at least an hour, or overnight.

2. Press Sauté and adjust it to high heat. Once the pot is hot, add the oil and half of the chicken thighs, skin side down. Brown the chicken for about 3-4 minutes. Turn them over and brown the other side for another 3-4 minutes. Remove the thighs onto a plate and set aside. Repeat with the second batch of chicken. Once the second batch is browned, return the first batch of chicken to the pot. Cancel Sauté mode.

3. Add the remaining ingredients.

4. Close and lock the lid, making sure the steam knob is on Sealing/Locked. Pressure cook on high pressure for 8 minutes.

5. Once the cooking is done, release the pressure by quick or natural pressure release.

6. Remove the chicken onto a serving platter. Press Sauté and adjust it to low. Simmer the sauce until thickened to desired consistency.

7. Pour the sauce over the chicken and serve with jasmine rice.

Cilantro Lime Chicken

This is probably one of the easiest recipes to put together. I converted this slow cooker recipe for the Instant Pot, resulting in all the flavour in less time. Cilantro lime chicken is perfect for burritos, tacos, or simply served with beans and rice.

Makes 4-6 servings

½ cup water
3 pound whole chicken
1 lime, halved
1 bunch of cilantro
4 cloves of garlic, smashed
salt and pepper

1. Place a trivet in the inner cooking pot. Add water.

2. Salt and pepper inside the cavity of the chicken. Fill the cavity with the cilantro and garlic. Place the chicken onto the trivet, breast-side up.

3. Squeeze lime juice over the chicken and toss the lime halves into the cavity of the chicken.   Be careful not to toss the lime into the pot as the rind of the lime will make the sauce bitter.

4. Close and lock the lid, making sure the steam knob is on Sealing/Locked. Pressure cook on high for 17 minutes (or 5.5 minutes per pound of chicken).

5. Once the cooking is done, release the pressure by quick pressure release.

6. Serve with rice, beans, salsa, guacamole and sour cream. Or shred the chicken to make burritos or tacos.

Portuguese Chicken

My mom made this dish a lot when I was teenager, using a bottled sauce. Over the last several years, portuguese chicken has been popping up on the menus at Hong Kong style cafés. I decided to recreate it at home. It's essentially a curry and I have adapted the recipe for the Instant Pot.

Makes 4-6 servings

6 skin-on, bone-in chicken thighs
2 tablespoons soy sauce
1 tablespoon ShaoHsing wine
1 tablespoon sugar
1 teaspoon grated fresh ginger
1 tablespoon cornstarch
1 tablespoon vegetable or canola oil
1 medium onion, sliced
1-2 cloves garlic, minced
6 small carrots, chopped into 1½ - 2 inch sized pieces
3 potatoes, chopped into 1½ - 2 inch sized pieces
1 teaspoon ground cumin
2 teaspoon turmeric
¾ cup chicken broth
1 can coconut milk (approximately 400ml)
1 tablespoon cornstarch
1 tablespoon cold water
salt to taste

———

1. In a large bowl, combine the chicken thighs, soy sauce, ShaoHsing wine, sugar, ginger and cornstarch and marinate for at least 30 minutes.

2. Press Sauté and adjust it to high heat. Once the pot is hot, add oil. Brown the chicken skin side down for about 3 minutes. Turn over and brown the other side, about 3 minutes. Remove to a plate and set aside. Discard the marinade.

3. Add onion and sauté until translucent, about 2 minutes. Add garlic and cook until fragrant, about 1 minute.

4. Add carrots and potatoes and cook for 2 minutes. Stir in cumin and turmeric and cook for another 1-2 minutes.

5. Pour in chicken broth, scraping the brown bits to deglaze, scraping up the brown

bits from the bottom of the pot as you go. Add coconut milk, chicken and any drippings.

6. Close and lock the lid, making sure the steam knob is on Sealing/Locked. Pressure cook on high for 8 minutes.

7. Once the cooking is done, quick release the pressure.

8. Press Sauté to simmer the sauce. In a small bowl, dissolve 1 tablespoon cornstarch in 1 tablespoon water and stir the slurry into the sauce. Heat through until sauce thickens. Season with salt to taste.

9. Serve with jasmine rice.

Thai Eggplant & Chicken Curry

This is a simple Thai red curry made with chicken and Thai eggplants. This round, golf ball sized, green and white eggplant is different from the purple eggplants and lengthy Japanese eggplants that we often find in the markets. They look more like tomatillos than their larger purple cousins. Because they are not always available, when I see them, I have to buy them. They soften easily while cooking, making them perfect for a tasty curry sauce.

Makes 6-8 servings

1 tablespoon vegetable or canola oil
3 tablespoons Thai red curry paste
13.5 ounce can coconut milk
6 boneless, skinless chicken thighs, cut
    into 1-2 inch pieces
2 tablespoons fish sauce
2 tablespoons sugar
¼ cup chicken stock
12 Thai eggplants, tops removed and
    halved
6 Thai basil leaves, chiffonade

———

1. Press Sauté and adjust to high heat. Once the pot is hot, add the curry paste and stir in 2 tablespoons of coconut milk. Add chicken and sauté for a few minutes.

2. Add the fish sauce, sugar, chicken stock, eggplants and remaining coconut milk and stir.

3. Close and lock the lid, making sure the steam knob is on Sealing/Locked. Pressure cook on high for 6 minutes.

4. Once the cooking is done, release the pressure by quick or natural pressure release.

5. Use the basil leaves as garnish or stir into the curry.

6. Serve with Jasmine rice.

You can use Japanese eggplant if you cannot find Thai eggplant. For more spiciness, increase the amount of curry paste or reduce the amount of coconut milk used.

Thai Yellow Curry with Chicken & Potato

We don't have many Thai restaurants in town, so I am thankful for the large variety of Thai curry pastes I can find in the Asian markets to make my own at home.

This recipe may seem very similar to the Thai Eggplant and Chicken Curry recipe. By changing the type of curry paste and one or two other ingredients will render a very different dish in flavour in textures.

Makes 4-6 servings

1 tablespoon vegetable or canola oil
3 tablespoon Thai yellow curry paste
13.5 ounce can coconut milk
6 boneless skinless chicken thighs, cut into 1-2 inch pieces
2 tablespoons fish sauce
2 tablespoons sugar
¼ cup chicken stock
1 pound baby potatoes, cut in half
6 Thai basil leaves, chiffonade

———

1. Press Sauté and adjust to high heat. Once the pot is hot, add the curry paste and a couple of tablespoons of coconut milk and stir. Add chicken and sauté for a few minutes.

2. Add the fish sauce, sugar, chicken stock, potatoes and remaining coconut milk and stir.

3. Close and lock the lid, making sure the steam knob is on Sealing/Locked. Pressure cook on high for 6 minutes.

4. Once the cooking is done, release the pressure by quick or natural pressure release.

5. Use the basil leaves as garnish or stir into the curry.

6. Serve with Jasmine rice.

Crustless Crab Frittata

Makes 4 servings

6 eggs
⅓ cup milk
½ pound fresh crab meat
2 green onions chopped
¼ teaspoon kosher salt
⅛ teaspoon fresh ground pepper
2 dashes hot pepper sauce (optional)
2 tablespoons freshly grated Parmesan

1. In a medium mixing bowl, whisk eggs until white and yolks are just combined. Do not over mix. Stir in the remaining ingredients.

2. Pour the mixture into a oven safe container that fits into the inner cooking pot. Using the pot-in-pot method, pour 1 cup of water into the inner cooking pot. Put the trivet in and place the container on top of the trivet.

3. Close and lock the lid, making sure the steam knob is on Sealing/Locked. Pressure cook on high for 20 minutes.

4. Once the cooking is done, let it natural pressure release for 10 minutes. Release the remaining pressure.

5. Place the frittata under the broiler for a few minutes to brown the top if desired (make sure your container is safe under the broiler).

6. Serve with a side salad.

Eggplant Parmesan

We are a family of carnivores but every now and then, I need a vegetarian option. I love eggplant and am always looking for ways to cook it so that the rest of the family will love it too. Flavourful dishes, whether they contain meat or not, are welcomed additions.

Makes 4 servings

1 large eggplant, cut into ½ inch thick
    rounds
2 tablespoons olive oil
2 cups freshly grated cheese
2 cups marinara sauce

1. Soak eggplant slices in water with a pinch of salt for 10 minutes. Use a plate as a weight to keep them submerged if necessary. Drain well. Heat up oil in a frying pan on medium heat. Brown the eggplant slices for about 3 minutes on each side. Season with salt and pepper. Drain on paper towels.

2. Line a 7-inch springform pan with parchment paper. Layer the eggplant, marinara sauce, and cheese. Repeat with remaining eggplant, sauce and cheese.

3. Using the pot-in-pot method, pour 1 cup of water into the inner cooking pot. Put the trivet in and place the springform pan on top of the trivet.

4. Close and lock the lid, making sure the steam knob is on Sealing/Locked. Pressure cook on high for 8 minutes.

5. Once the cooking is done, quick or natural pressure release.

6. Place the pan under the broiler for a few minutes to brown the top if desired (make sure your pan is safe under the broiler).

7. There may be a lot of liquid in the pan. Place the pan on a serving platter and carefully remove from the springform pan or slice servings directly from the pan.

Motel Pasta

This is called motel pasta because I first put it together while we were staying in a motel during one of our road trips. When I was a kid, my mom always packed the rice cooker on our family road trips. She would make rice, chicken-in-a-can and napa cabbage. The chicken came whole, stuffed in a can with broth. My mom would make the rice first, scoop it out and then pour the can of chicken into the rice cooker along with the cabbage to heat through and that would be dinner. Ingenious, right?!

Technology and techniques may have a changed since then but we now travel with the Instant Pot to accomplish a similar goal - to save money and to provide a nutritious meal for the family (minus the chicken-in-a-can).

Makes 4-6 servings

1 pound of pasta
4 cups of water and 1 tablespoon chicken bouillon or 4 cups of chicken broth
1 cup mascarpone or cream cheese
½ cup milk
salt and pepper to taste
4 cups shredded cooked chicken
½ pound arugula

---

1. Add the pasta to the inner cooking pot and add water and bouillon, or broth, until pasta is just covered.

2. Close and lock the lid, making sure the steam knob is on Sealing/Locked. Pressure cook on high for half the amount of time provided on the package instructions (i.e. if the package says to cook for 8 minutes, cook for 4 minutes in the electric pressure cooker).

3. Once the cooking is done, quick release the pressure.

4. Press Sauté. Add cheese, milk, and salt and pepper to taste. Stir until cheese melts. Add chicken and heat through.

5. Cancel Sauté mode. Add arugula and stir until wilted. Serve immediately.

One-Pot Pasta Bolognese

This is probably my favourite go to Instant Pot recipe. What's not to like about a rich Bolognese sauce, infused with bacon goodness? I used to make this recipe on the stove top, in my trusty cast iron pot and boil the pasta in a separate pot. Being able to prepare the sauce and pasta in one-pot, in the Instant Pot, has allowed me to prepare a speedy meal with deep flavours.

If I am in a hurry, I might omit the bacon, but truly, the bacon is everything!

Makes 4-6 servings

1 pound bacon
1 pound lean ground beef or ground sweet Italian sausage
1 medium onion, chopped
3 cups beef broth or water
1 pound pasta
24 ounce jar of tomato and basil sauce or marinara sauce

———

1. Press Sauté, and adjust it to high heat. Once the pot is hot, add the bacon and render until brown. Remove the bacon and drain on a paper towel.

2. Leave 2 tablespoons of bacon fat in the pot. Add the onion and cook for 2 minutes. Add the beef or sausage and cook until browned. Pour in the beef broth and deglaze, scraping up the brown bits from the bottom of the pot as you go.

3. Add the pasta and do not stir. If you are using spaghetti, try to fan out the noodles so that it looks like pick-up sticks. This will help keep the pasta from clumping.

4. Cover the pasta with the tomato sauce.

5. Close and lock the lid, making sure the steam knob is on Sealing/Locked. Choose manual high pressure for half the amount of cook time stated on the package of pasta. (i.e. if the package says to cook for 8 minutes, cook for 4 minutes in the electric pressure cooker).

6. Once the pasta is done, quick release the pressure. The pasta will look soupy. Give the pasta a good stir and the pasta will absorb the rest of the liquid. Serve immediately.

Apple Bacon Pork Shoulder

Pork shoulder is an inexpensive piece of meat and when it's cooked well, it is tender and full of flavour. I especially enjoy making this in the Fall because the ingredients scream autumn to me but it can be made and enjoyed anytime of year.

Makes 6-8 servings

12 ounces bacon, cut into ½ inch pieces
3 pounds pork shoulder roast, cut into 3-4 large cubes
2 large onions, cut into large pieces
½ cup chicken broth
3 sprigs fresh thyme or ¾ teaspoon dried thyme
2 firm apples (e.g. fuji, honeycrisp, ambrosia) peeled, cored and sliced thinly
1 tablespoon cornstarch
1 tablespoon water
1 tablespoon Italian parsley, chopped
salt and pepper to taste

———

1. Press Sauté, and adjust it to high heat. Once the pot is hot, add the bacon and render until brown. Remove the bacon and drain on a paper towel.

2. Leave 2 tablespoons of bacon fat in the pot and brown the pork shoulder for about 2 minutes on each side.

3. Remove the pork shoulder onto a plate. Add onions and sauté for a couple of minutes. Add the chicken stock and deglaze, scraping up the brown bits from the bottom of the pot as you go. Return the pork shoulder to the pot and add thyme. Cancel Sauté mode.

4. Close and lock the lid, making sure the steam knob is on Sealing/Locked. Pressure cook on high for 45 minutes.

5. Once the cooking is done, release the pressure by quick or natural pressure release.

6. Skim the fat from the top. Press Sauté and remove the pork to a serving plate. Add the apples. Reduce the sauce, cooking for about 5 minutes.

7. In a small bowl, dissolve the cornstarch in the water and stir the slurry into the sauce. Heat through until sauce thickens. If it's not thick enough, add another mixture of slurry. Salt and pepper to taste.

8. Pour the sauce over the pork shoulder, garnish with bacon and chopped parsley.

Asian Braised Pork Shoulder

I generally prefer Asian flavours for pork. This is one of the first recipes I tried in the Instant Pot. I was so impressed by how wonderfully flavourful and tender the pork was, especially after such a short time, compared to slowly cooking in the oven for hours.

Makes 6-8 servings

3 pounds pork shoulder roast, cut into 3-4 even pieces
1 teaspoon kosher salt
2 tablespoons olive oil
5 cloves garlic, minced
1 tablespoon grated fresh ginger
¼ cup soy sauce
½ cup rice vinegar
¼ cup chicken stock
¼ cup oyster sauce
½ cup brown sugar
3 star anise (optional)
1-2 tablespoons cilantro, chopped for garnish

Instead of pork shoulder roast, use pork shoulder bone-in steaks. Follow the same recipe except cut the cooking time down to 20 minutes.

1. Press Sauté and adjust it to high heat. Season each piece of pork with salt. Once the pot is hot, add the olive oil and brown the pork for about 3-4 minutes a side. Remove the pork and set aside on a plate. Add the garlic and ginger to the pot and sauté for about 30-60 seconds until fragrant.

2. Pour in the soy sauce and rice wine vinegar and simmer until reduced by half. Cancel Sauté mode. Stir in the chicken stock, oyster sauce, brown sugar and star anise (if using). Return the pork to the pot.

3. Close and lock the lid, making sure the steam knob is on Sealing/Locked. Pressure cook on high for 45 minutes.

4. Once the cooking is done, release the pressure by quick or natural pressure release.

5. Remove the pork onto a serving platter. Press Sauté and adjust it to high heat. Simmer the sauce until thickened. Drizzle the sauce over the pork, garnish with cilantro and serve with jasmine rice.

Carnitas

We really miss authentic Mexican food from our time in the San Francisco Bay Area. Since we don't have as many options in Vancouver, I have experimented with cooking Mexican at home. Here is a super easy pork carnitas recipe for the Instant Pot and it has become one of my son's favourite meals!

Makes 6-8 servings

2 pounds pork shoulder roast, cut into 2 inch cubes
1 bay leaf
4 garlic cloves, smashed
1 tablespoon kosher salt
1 cup of water

1. Combine all the ingredients in the inner cooking pot.

2. Close and lock the lid, making sure the steam knob is on Sealing/Locked. Pressure cook on high for 45 minutes.

3. Once the cooking is done, release the pressure by quick or natural pressure release.

4. Brown the meat by using either of these methods. Option 1: Heat up a frying pan and add 1 tablespoon oil. Dry the pieces of pork with paper towels and fry until nicely browned on one side and turn over to brown the other side. Option 2: Spread the meat out on a sheet pan and place under broiler for 3-5 minutes or until nicely browned. Turn them over and brown the other side.

5. Serve with rice, beans, salsa, guacamole and sour cream. You can also use carnitas to make burritos or tacos.

Barbecue Ribs

There are a number of ways to prepare ribs and everyone has their favourite way of making them. I used to either boil them for an hour and then bake them for another hour, or I would slow-cook them in the oven for 3-4 hours. Cooking them in the Instant Pot has easily become my favourite way to make ribs. Now, I can have tender and juicy ribs for dinner any night of the week, in less than an hour from start to finish.

Makes 4-6 servings

2 full racks of pork back ribs
kosher salt
1 cup water
Bottle of your favourite barbecue sauce

SAUCE INGREDIENTS (optional)
1½ cup ketchup
½ cup barbecue sauce
½ cup brown sugar
juice from ½ lemon
1 teaspoon Worcestershire sauce
2 tablespoons steak sauce
1 clove minced garlic
dash of hot sauce (to taste or optional)

Sometimes I try a new barbecue sauce that I don't particularly like so instead of wasting the sauce, I use it as a base to create a new sauce by adding other ingredients.

1. Season ribs with salt and place in the inner cooking pot. Add 1 cup of water.

2. Close and lock the lid, making sure the steam knob is on Sealing/Locked. Pressure cook on high for 18 minutes. If you like the ribs less fall-off-the-bone, with a little tug on them, cook them for only 15 minutes or if you want them to completely fall off the bone, cook for 20 minutes.

3. If you are making the sauce, combine all sauce ingredients in a small pot and cook on medium heat for 20 minutes.

4. Once the ribs are done, quick release the pressure. Remove the ribs and place on a sheet pan. You can either slather the sauce over the full racks of ribs with a basting brush or separate the ribs and baste each one with sauce. Place under the broiler until the sauce begins to caramelize (approximately 5-8 minutes). Alternatively, the ribs can be finished off on the grill.

Pork Adobo

Makes 4-6 servings

5-6 pounds pork back ribs, cut into ribs
¾ cup soy sauce
½ cup vinegar
2 tablespoons sugar
2 teaspoons whole peppercorn
2 bay leaves
10 cloves garlic, smashed

---

1. Rinse the ribs and soak them in cold water for about an hour to remove excess blood and impurities.

2. Layer the ribs in the inner cooking pot. Add the remaining ingredients.

3. Close and lock the lid, making sure the steam knob is on Sealing/Locked. Pressure cook on manual high pressure for 15 minutes.

4. Once the cooking is done, release the pressure by quick or natural pressure release.

5. Press Sauté and adjust it to low. Simmer the sauce until the sauce thickens and occasionally stir the ribs around as the ribs will darken from the sauce.

6. Serve with jasmine rice.

Chinese Sticky Rice

The past generations in my family did not write down a single recipe. Somehow they just knew how much of each ingredient to use. I'd love to be able to pass on the tradition and tastes of the homemade dishes I grew up with. Thankfully, we have a 'world wide web' full of techniques and recipes to help us create family recipes that can be passed on to future generations.

Chinese Sticky Rice was my great aunt's specialty. She would bring it to our Christmas family gathering every year. One year, instead of making it, she bought it from a local restaurant. Of course, everyone knew there was something not quite right. She never pulled that one on us again.

Makes 6-8 servings

3 cups glutinous rice, soaked in cold water for at least 1 hour and drained
6 dried scallops, soaked in cold water overnight
2 ounces dried shrimp, soaked in hot water for 10 minutes
5-6 Chinese sausages
1 strip preserved pork belly
6 fresh shiitake mushrooms

5-6 green onion
3 tablespoon vegetable or canola oil, divided
2-3 tablespoon soy sauce

Glutinous rice is also labelled as sweet rice. Blanching the pork belly will make it easier to cut.

---

1. Prepare all your ingredients. Shred the scallops, reserving the liquid. Drain the shrimp, reserving the liquid. Chop Chinese sausages, pork belly, and mushrooms into 1/4 inch cubes. Finely chop green onions, separating white and light green parts from dark green parts.

2. Press Sauté. Once the pot is hot, add 2 tablespoon oil. Add Chinese sausage, pork belly, mushrooms and white and light parts of green onions and stir fry for 2-3 minutes.

3. Stir in the rice until it is coated with the oil. Add scallops and shrimp and mix well. Cancel Sauté mode.

4. In a large liquid measuring cup, add the liquid from the shrimp and scallops, soy sauce and enough water amounting to 4 cups of liquid.

5. Close and lock the lid, making sure the steam knob is on Sealing/Locked. Pressure cook on high for 4 minutes. Once the cooking is done, let it natural pressure release for 10 minutes. Release the remaining pressure.

6. Stir in green parts of green onion. Serve immediately.

Steamed Egg

This is a childhood favourite and brings back many memories and feelings of nostalgia. When we were kids, we would fight over who got to "lick the bowl". There would always be just a little left and the kid who called dibs would get to add a small scoop of rice and soak up the remaining soft and creamy goodness and eat it right from the serving bowl… simple pleasures.

Makes 2-4 servings

4 eggs
12 half shells of chicken broth or cooled boiled water (ratio egg to water 1:1.5)
1 teaspoon soy sauce
1/2 teaspoon sesame oil
pinch ground white pepper
1 green onion, chopped

1. Beat eggs and water in a bowl. Pour into oven safe bowl that will fit inside your pressure cooker. Cover with foil or a silicone lid.

2. Add 1 cup of water in your pressure cooker. Place the covered bowl on top of a trivet.

3. Close and lock the lid, making sure the steam knob is on Sealing/Locked. Pressure cook on high for 8 minutes.

4. Once the cooking is done, quick release the pressure.

5. Drizzle with soy sauce and sesame oil. Sprinkle white pepper and green onions.

6. Serve with rice.

Desserts

Applesauce
Crème Caramel
Lemon Cheesecake with Shortbread Crust

Applesauce

There was always applesauce in the fridge when I was growing up. My grandmother would gather all the overripe or bruised apples that could not be sold in our grocery store and use those for applesauce.

When the kids were babies, I made it for them too, without the added flavours. They still enjoy applesauce to this day and will ask for it every now and then. It's so much faster with the Instant Pot.

Makes 4-6 cups

8 apples peeled, cored and cut into 1-1½ inch pieces
1 tablespoon fresh lemon juice
¼ cup water
½ teaspoon ground cinnamon
¼ cup brown sugar

1. Place all the ingredients in the inner cooking pot.

2. Close and lock the lid, making sure the steam knob is on Sealing/Locked. Pressure cook on high for 4 minutes.

3. Once the cooking is done, let it natural pressure release.

4. Serve as is or process with hand blender or food processor to desired texture.

Crème Caramel

Crème caramel is one of my favourite desserts. I first made this crème caramel in the Instant Pot for our French hosts while visiting the South of France. This is a very simple recipe to make as it only has four ingredients! I love to see and taste the specks of vanilla in the custard.

Makes 6-8 servings

CUSTARD
2 cups whole milk
1 vanilla bean (or 2 teaspoons vanilla extract)
4 eggs
⅔ cup sugar

CARAMEL
½ cup sugar
1 tablespoons water

---

1. Slice down the middle of the vanilla bean lengthwise and use the back of your knife to scrape out the seeds.

2. Heat milk, vanilla bean seeds, and vanilla bean pod in a small saucepan on medium heat, just until simmering. Set aside and let cool.

3. In a separate saucepan, heat ½ cup sugar and 1 tablespoon water on medium high heat until caramel turns a deep amber colour, occasionally swirling your sugar. Keep watch and take it off the heat when it's done, approximately 5-7 minutes, otherwise it will burn.

4. Slowly pour the caramel, coating the bottom and the sides of a oven safe bowl that will fit into the inner cooking pot. The caramel will harden as it cools so you will need to work quickly.

5. In a medium bowl, beat eggs and ⅔ cup sugar. Remove the pod from the milk and slowly add the warm milk to the eggs. Temper the eggs by pouring the milk slowly, just in case it's too hot. You don't want to scramble the eggs.

6. Pour the egg mixture over the hardened caramel. Cover tightly with foil or with a silicone lid.

7. Place a trivet in the inner cooking pot and add 1 cup of water. Place the covered bowl on top of a trivet.

8. Close and lock the lid, making sure the steam knob is on Sealing/Locked. Pressure cook on high for 10 minutes.

9. Once the cooking is done, let it natural pressure release for 10 minutes.

10. Release the rest of the pressure and check for doneness. Stick a toothpick in the centre and it should come out clean. The custard should be set but still a bit jiggly.

11. Remove the bowl and let cool for 1 hour. Then chill in the refrigerator for at least 3 hours.

12. After the custard has chilled, run a spatula around the inside edge of the bowl. Place your serving platter with lip on top of the bowl, while tightly holding the plate and bowl together, carefully flip the bowl over upside down. The sauce will pool on the plate.

Lemon Cheesecake with Shortbread Crust

Making cheesecake in the Instant Pot is much easier and faster than baking it in a water bath in the oven. I enjoy a shortbread crust, but you can also use a traditional graham cracker crust.

Makes 6-8 servings

SHORTBREAD CRUST
½ cup butter, room temperature
¼ cup sugar
1 cup flour

CHEESECAKE FILLING
8 ounce package cream cheese, room temperature
½ cup sugar
1 cup sour cream
1 egg
zest of 1 lemon
2 tablespoons lemon juice
1 teaspoon vanilla extract

———

1. Preheat oven to 400°F.

2. Cream together butter and sugar in the bowl of an electric mixer. Scrape down the sides and add the flour. Mix until crumbly.

3. Press the crumb mixture into a 7 x 3 inch springform pan and refrigerate for 10 minutes. Bake in preheated oven for 15 minutes.

4. Let the crust cool completely before adding cheesecake filling.

5. With an electric mixer on medium, beat cream cheese until smooth. Add sugar in a steady stream.

6. For the next few steps, only mix for 30 seconds and make sure to scrape down the side after the addition of each ingredient.

    • Add half the sour cream, mix for 30 seconds and scrape the sides of the bowl-down. Repeat with remaining sour cream.
    • Add the egg.
    • Add the lemon zest and lemon juice.
    • Add the vanilla.

7. Pour the batter into the cooled crust. Tap pan on work surface to remove any air bubbles. Cover tightly with foil or with a silicone lid.

8. Place a trivet in the inner cooking pot and add 1 cup of water. Place the covered cheesecake on top of the trivet.

9. Close and lock the lid, making sure the steam knob is on Sealing/Locked. Pressure cook on high for 35 minutes

10. Once the cooking is done, let it natural pressure release for 10 minutes. The cheesecake should be mostly set, with only the center slightly jiggly.

11. Remove the pan and let it cool for an hour and refrigerate overnight or for at least 4 hours.

Index

Made in the USA
Monee, IL
31 August 2020